BURMESE PYTHONS

BY EMILY ROSE OACHS

EPIC

BELLWETHER MEDIA • MINNEAPOLIS, MN

EPIC BOOKS are no ordinary books. They burst with intense action, high-speed heroics, and shadows of the unknown. Are you ready for an Epic adventure?

This edition first published in 2014 by Bellwether Media, Inc.

No part of this publication may be reproduced in whole or in part without written permission of the publisher. For information regarding permission, write to Bellwether Media, Inc., Attention: Permissions Department, 5357 Penn Avenue South, Minneapolis, MN 55419.

Library of Congress Cataloging-in-Publication Data

Oachs, Emily Rose.
  Burmese Pythons / by Emily Rose Oachs.
     pages cm. – (Epic: Amazing Snakes!)
  Includes bibliographical references and index.
  Summary: "Engaging images accompany information about Burmese pythons. The combination of high-interest subject matter and light text is intended for students in grades 2 through 7"– Provided by publisher.
  Audience: Ages 7-12
  ISBN 978-1-62617-089-6 (hardcover : alk. paper)
  1. Burmese python–Juvenile literature. I. Title.
  QL666.O67O34 2014
  597.96'78–dc23
                        2013034259

Printed in the United States of America, North Mankato, MN.

TABLE OF CONTENTS

WHAT ARE BURMESE PYTHONS?

Burmese pythons are among the largest snakes in the world. They measure up to 23 feet (7 meters) long. Some weigh 200 pounds (90 kilograms)!

6

These snakes have tan skin with brown and black spots. Dark lines cross their eyes. This pattern camouflages them in the wild.

Pale Pythons

Burmese pythons can also be yellow with white markings. This coloring is mostly found in pet Burmese pythons.

WHERE BURMESE PYTHONS LIVE

N
W   E
S

burmese python range =

Burmese pythons live in southeastern Asia. They make their homes in marshes, grasslands, and jungles.

New in Town

Some people brought Burmese pythons to Florida as pets. Now these massive snakes also live in the Everglades!

Burmese pythons are often found near water. They are skilled swimmers. They can stay underwater for 30 minutes!

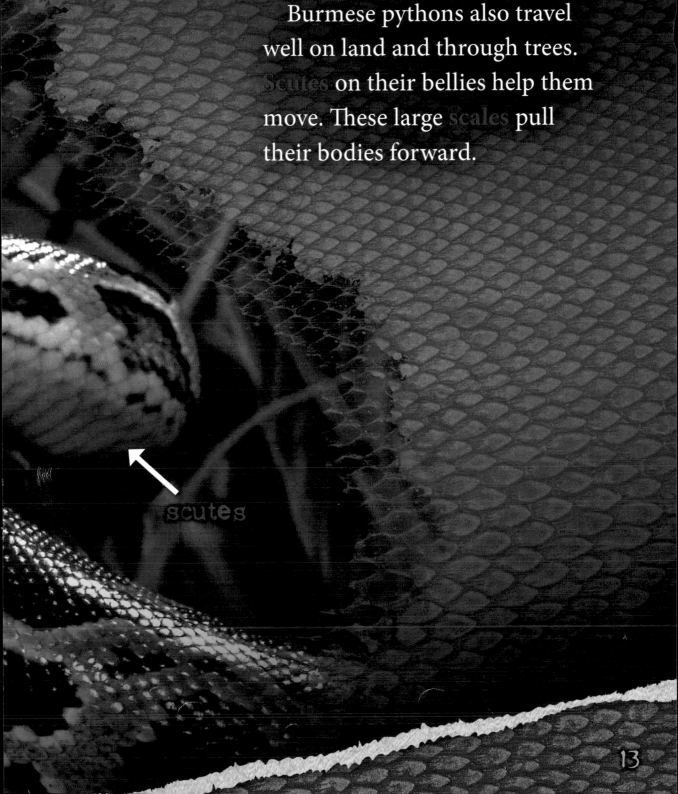

Burmese pythons also travel well on land and through trees. Scutes on their bellies help them move. These large scales pull their bodies forward.

scutes

HUNTING FOR PREY

Burmese
Python
Prey

Full Bellies
Burmese pythons can go months without eating.

Burmese pythons use forked tongues and pits on their faces to find prey. They hunt for birds, mice, lizards, and rabbits. Some even go after leopards!

A Burmese python attacks its
meal. Its sharp teeth hold the animal
down. Then its body coils around
the prey. The Burmese python
constricts its catch.

Get a Grip

A Burmese python's teeth
point backward. This
helps it grip its prey.

Burmese pythons can swallow animals larger than their heads!

The Burmese python opens its flexible jaws wide. Slowly, the python swallows its dinner whole.

SPECIES PROFILE

SCIENTIFIC NAME:	*PYTHON MOLURUS BIVITTATUS*
AVERAGE SIZE:	16-23 FEET (5-7 METERS)
HABITATS:	JUNGLES, MARSHES, GRASSLANDS
COUNTRIES:	BANGLADESH, CAMBODIA, CHINA, INDIA, INDONESIA, LAOS, MYANMAR, NEPAL, THAILAND, UNITED STATES, VIETNAM
VENOMOUS:	NO
HUNTING METHOD:	CONSTRICTION
COMMON PREY:	BIRDS, MICE, RABBITS, LIZARDS, LEOPARDS

GLOSSARY

camouflages—hides an animal or thing by helping it blend in with the surroundings

coils—winds or wraps around something

constricts—squeezes until breathing stops

flexible—able to stretch

marshes—grassy wetlands

pits—heat-sensing holes around the mouth; Burmese pythons use pits to hunt for food at night.

prey—animals that are hunted by other animals for food

scales—small plates of skin that cover and protect a snake's body

scutes—large, rough scales on the stomach of a snake

TO LEARN MORE

At the Library

Cheng, Christopher. *Python*. Somerville, Mass.: Candlewick Press, 2013.

Clark, Willow. *Burmese Pythons*. New York, N.Y.: PowerKids Press, 2013.

Sexton, Colleen. *Pythons*. Minneapolis, Minn.: Bellwether Media, 2010.

On the Web

Learning more about Burmese pythons is as easy as 1, 2, 3.

1. Go to www.factsurfer.com.

2. Enter "Burmese pythons" into the search box.

3. Click the "Surf" button and you will see a list of related Web sites.

With factsurfer.com, finding more information is just a click away.

INDEX